A COMPLIMENTARY REVIEW COPY, SPRING 1970

A HOLIDAY BOOK

Christmas in Britain and Scandinavia

...elebrations
...les are de-
...ul of holi-
...tivals and
...gious cus-
...ake these
HOLIDAY
...g readers
...through
...nner.

...h elemen-
...tary school teacher and librarian, is now a specialist in the Bureau of Library Services for the Baltimore, Maryland public schools. She spends much of her time training librarians and teachers and helping them to learn new ways of bringing children and books together. Miss Patterson has degrees from Hampton Institute and Catholic University and has done further study at several other colleges and universities. She has written nine other books for Garrard, including five HOLIDAY BOOKS, two of which are about Christmas.

Reading Level: Grade 3   Interest Level: Grades 2–5
64 pages . . . 8 x 9½   Publisher's Price: $2.59

SBN 8116-6564-X

Illustrated with photographs; full-color jacket; reinforced binding

GARRARD PUBLISHING COMPANY

Christmas
in Britain and Scandinavia

BY LILLIE PATTERSON
ILLUSTRATED BY KELLY OECHSLI

1305

GARRARD PUBLISHING COMPANY
CHAMPAIGN, ILLINOIS

For

Elizabeth McCombs and Evelyn Matthews

Holiday books are edited under
the educational supervision of

Charles E. Johnson, Ed.D.
Professor of Education
University of Georgia

Acknowledgements:

Excerpt on page 58 is from Dylan Thomas, *Quite Early One Morning.* Copyright 1954 by New Directions Publishing Corporation. Reprinted by permission of New Directions Publishing Corporation.

Picture credits:

Bettmann Archive: p. 42
British Travel Association, London: p. 47 (both)
Danish Information Office, New York: p. 4, 13 (top left and right), 25
Finnish Ministry of Foreign Affairs, Helsinki: p. 35, 36
Finnish National Travel Office, New York: p. 38
Irish Tourist Board, New York: p. 62, 64
Norwegian National Travel Office, New York: p. 8, 13 (bottom), 17, 19
Radio Times Hulton Picture Library, London: p. 50, 52
Scottish Tourist Board, Edinburgh: p. 57
Swedish Information Service, New York: p. 31 (top right and bottom)
Swedish National Travel Office, New York: p. 1, 31 (top left)

Contents

1. The Story of *Jul*

Jul, Christmas in Scandinavia, is the year's biggest, gayest, and longest festival. Early in December figures of mischievous red-capped gnomes, called *Julenisser*, begin to appear in Norway, Denmark, Sweden, and Finland. Other popular holiday decorations include goats, pigs, evergreens, and white lights.

These symbols date back to ancient festivals much older than Christmas. People living in northern lands like Scandinavia and Britain feared winter's darkness as a time of mystery. Dead souls roamed abroad. Evil spirits that dwelled in cold, dark places had power to bring floods, storms, poor crops, and other ills.

Only the gods of nature could battle and control these spirits. The Northmen planned gay midwinter festivals to honor their nature gods, especially their beloved sun gods. Their new year began at the winter solstice, when the "new sun" began to grow stronger, and the days longer.

Clothes, homes, even people themselves were made freshly clean to welcome the returning sun and the new year. Evil spirits could not live in cleanliness or near evergreens, so people decorated their homes and clothing with evergreens. They rejoiced, sang, feasted, and held many ceremonies using light and fire.

The name for this northern festival has been traced to many origins. One is the Germanic word, *hweol*, meaning wheel, symbol of the turning point of the year. Another is an Old English word, *geola*, meaning feast. Whatever its beginning, the name came down in the English language as Yule, and in Scandinavia as *Joulu* or *Jul*.

The Norsemen, or Vikings, as the early Scandinavians were called, worshipped a sun god called Frey. He ruled over crops and trees. Frey rode across the sky from east to west each day in a chariot drawn by a golden boar. Norsemen honored Frey by feasting on roasted boar's head, and rolling blazing wheels into the sea. They also honored Thor, god of thunder and rain. Thor streaked across the sky in a chariot drawn by two goats.

Jul slowly changed after the Christian faith reached Scandinavia in about the ninth century. The pagan festival became a Christian feast honoring Jesus' birth. The change was easy because missionaries let the people adapt their pagan rites to Christian rejoicing. Pagan fires changed to Jul logs and candlelight ceremonies. Thor's goat was made a symbol of the season's joy and plenty. Frey's boar became the "Christmas pig" for feasts. Many rituals were banned by the Church but survived in the form of children's games.

Sometimes Father dresses up like Julenisse.

Superstitious beliefs took on new forms too. The evil spirits shrank to tiny, magical beings, such as the nisse. This gnome lives in dark places—cellars, attics, haylofts—but he brings good luck, not harm, into homes. He dearly loves cats and children.

The nisse can be mischievous, though, and play tricks. Families may awake one morning and find dishes cracked, or the horses' manes tied in knots. They have to bribe the nisse into being good with a bowl of porridge, his favorite food.

In modern years the nisse has captured the imagination of the children. As the popularity of St. Nicholas, Father Christmas, and Santa Claus grew, Scandinavians wanted an exciting gift-bringer, too. Since the nisse dressed in red and had a long white beard, he was perfect for the role. He became the Julenisse.

Julenisse brings gifts to children in Norway and Denmark. A similar gnome, *Jultomten*, comes to Sweden. On Christmas Eve children place a bowl of porridge in the barn, attic, or kitchen to remind the Christmas gnomes to bring presents.

Advent, the four-week period of preparation for Christmas, is a busy time in Scandinavia. Housewives, famed for their pastries, often bake as many as fourteen different kinds of holiday cookies. Children delight in cutting cookies into shapes of gnomes, goats, pigs, stars, bells, and people. Gingerbread goats and pigs are made by the dozens, and a gingerbread castle is the joy of every child.

Fancy candlesticks are polished until they shine. Houses are thoroughly cleaned, then decorated with evergreens and real flowers. Scandinavians love flowers and grow them in pots on their windowsills. Favorite Christmas flowers are begonias, roses, red tulips, and white hyacinths.

Christmas Eve is the most important day of the season. In late afternoon church bells ring in "the peace of Jul." Sometimes snow falls in big flakes, adding to the loveliness of the white lights used in decorations.

Church bells call families to Christmas services. Although there are now many cars, some farm families still travel to the Christmas services in horse-drawn sleighs. The horses prance, and the sleigh bells jingle merrily.

After church some families visit cemeteries nearby and decorate graves of loved ones and heroes. Every grave has a candle, a small Christmas tree, or a wreath. Candles flicker across the snow while church bells chime.

The home celebration begins that evening with a reading of the story of Jesus' birth from the Bible. This is followed by the biggest feast of the year. Long ago, people believed that the bigger the feast, the better their luck in the coming year.

The feast begins with two traditional dishes, *lutefisk* and rice porridge. Lutefisk is dried codfish served with white sauce. The custom of eating fish came from the time when Christmas Eve was a fast day. One serving of the porridge always contains an almond. Whoever finds it is supposed to have good luck all year.

"Every part of the pig is used except the squeal," housewives say jokingly. Along with the roast pork or ham, they serve sausages, spareribs, chops, and pickled pig's feet, called pig's trotters. A pig's head with an apple in its mouth is still seen on some tables.

After dinner the family gathers around the Christmas tree. Every home has a tree, for forests of spruce, fir, and pine are plentiful in Scandinavia. Many families still use real candles on their trees, as their soft glow is so peaceful.

Children cut out many of the tree decorations from paper. Paper chains, nisser, hearts, stars, pigs, goats, angels, and birds fairly dance along the branches. Cookies, apples, nuts, and baskets of sweets are hung with the decorations. Modern "Christmas flares" send out a bright shower of sparks when lighted.

Small flags are strung together and looped across branches, and a larger flag sometimes adorns the top. Each country uses not only its own flag, but also flags of other nations.

Although children make tree decorations, mothers and fathers usually trim the trees and keep them hidden behind locked doors. The most exciting moment of Jul comes when the door swings open to reveal the lighted tree.

Everyone in the family joins hands to dance around it and sing carols. A favorite song is

Jul is the time for bringing home a
Christmas tree and adorning it with
real candles, bright ornaments and
little Scandinavian flags.

the Swedish dance carol, *"Nu Ar Det Jul Igen,"* "Now It's Christmas Again."

> Now it's Christmas again, Christmas again,
> We'll dance and celebrate till Easter.
> Then, when it's Easter time,
> Yes, then, when it's Easter time,
> We'll dance and celebrate till Christmas.

Suddenly Julenisse or Jultomten appears, played by the father, an uncle, older brother, or a neighbor. This big Julenisse or "Christmas Man" looks like a combination of Father Christmas and Santa Claus, but wears the mask of a gnome.

Christmas Eve closes with a lovely wish: "May God bless your Christmas. May it last till Easter."

December 25, called First Christmas Day, begins with church services. This is a day for quiet family reunions. Visiting and parties start on December 26, Second Christmas Day.

Epiphany, January 6, is called "Day of the

Three Kings." Three-pronged candles are lighted to honor the kings who followed the Star to Bethlehem. "Star boys" may still be seen parading with lighted stars atop tall poles. Sometimes they masquerade as Bible characters and wear peaked hats decorated with stars. At least one boy may carry a toy goat as the singing group moves from house to house asking for treats.

Holiday fun continues until King Knut's Day, January 13. King Knut was the ruler who set aside twenty days for celebrating Jul. Families remember him by lighting trees and candles for the last time on his feast day.

> The twentieth day, King Knut did rule,
> Should end the festival of Jul.

These modern customs are common to all Scandinavian countries, though they may vary from section to section. In addition, each country developed some unusual customs that grew out of its own history.

2. Norway

"The Advent calendars are here!" Norwegian children shout. Each morning they open a tiny window or door on their calendars to see a new picture, reminding them of the holiday season ahead. Advent calendars are popular with all Scandinavian children.

As Advent advances, children help to bake the *Julekake,* which is Christmas cake—filled with raisins, citron, and currants. Tiny dough-nuts, small almond cakes, pepper cookies, and *Berlinerkranser* are traditional holiday sweets. Berlinerkranser or "Berliner Wreaths" are cookies baked in the shape of wreaths that glitter with crushed sugar.

Norwegians cannot imagine Christmas without a tree, a spruce if possible. Seamen and fishermen even tie trees to the mastheads of their ships.

During World War II when German troops occupied Norway, Norway's King Haakon escaped to Britain. At Christmastime, a small Norwegian ship stationed in England stole

past the German naval patrol into a Norwegian harbor and brought a spruce tree back to England. King Haakon was able to enjoy a real Norwegian Christmas. The custom continued, and each Christmas Norwegians send a tree to Britain as a gift of goodwill.

Holiday preparations are finished by *Julaften,* Christmas Eve. Farm animals are given extra portions of the finest oats or barley, along with an old greeting: "It is Julaften, good friend. Eat well."

Sheaves of grain, *Julenek*, set atop tall poles make treats for sparrows and other winter birds. Grain sheaves swing from housetops, apartment balconies, fences, and porches. Bits of bread, suet, or grain are spread on windowsills, or hung on branches to make birds' Christmas trees. The lovely custom of giving "gifts" to animals and birds is popular all over Scandinavia.

At family feasts, a moment of suspense comes when each person dips into his Christmas porridge. The lucky person who finds the almond also gets an extra gift. Mothers sometimes slip a raisin in another serving. The unlucky raisin-finder must be the "slavey" for the evening—washing the dishes, or doing tasks family members demand.

By the time dinner ends, young children are nearly exploding with excitement. At last the locked door swings open, and children rush in to see their lighted tree. Excitement grows even greater when a loud knock is heard, and Julenisse enters with his bag of gifts. Skis

are popular presents in Scandinavia. Children as young as four get their first pair. Skates, sleds, mittens, sweaters, hoods, and scarves are gifts useful during the long holidays.

Christmas morning often begins with a special snack. Norwegian mothers and fathers serve currant juice or hot chocolate, buns, and cookies to their children in bed. *"God Jul!"* or *"Gledelig Jul!"* they call out wishes for a Happy Christmas. Christmas Day is a time for quiet family reunions.

The next day begins the long season of fun and hospitality. Christmas tree parties delight young children. Tables are decorated with small trees, and children wear colorful paper hats shaped like crowns or like Julenisse caps.

Julebukk, Christmas buck parties, are fun for the older children. Julebukk customs were passed down from Viking festivals. In olden days, a person would dress up in a goatskin, carry a goat's head, and burst in upon a party of merrymakers. He pretended to die and be brought back to life, symbolizing the sun's rebirth.

Today's Julebukk game is similar to the Halloween "trick or treat." Children dress in ridiculous costumes and go singing from house to house looking for treats. Some children masquerade as goats, or carry toy goats with them.

Norwegian greetings change as the season advances. After Christmas Day it becomes *"Fortsatt God Jul,"* "Continued Happy Christmas." When Jul ends on Epiphany or on King Knut's Day, a final greeting is exchanged. *"Jul vel overstatt"* means "I hope you had a happy Christmas."

3. Denmark

"Far out in the forest grew a pretty little fir tree." So begins "The Fir Tree" by Hans Christian Andersen. The fairy tale tells how the little fir grew to be a big beautiful tree, and was gloriously decorated one Christmas, for children. Andersen was born in Denmark and he knew how much the Danes love Jul and fir trees.

On *Juleaften*, Christmas Eve, the family feast is as gay as the red and white decorations so loved by Danes. The meat of honor is roast goose or duck, stuffed with apples and prunes, and decorated with a small red and white Danish flag.

After dinner everyone chooses a favorite carol to sing around the Christmas tree. Someone is sure to choose the traditional Danish carol, "A Child Is Born in Bethlehem."

A Child is born in Bethlehem,
In Bethlehem;
And joy is in Jerusalem,
Alleluia, alleluia!

The singing heralds the welcome of Julenisse with his bag of gifts. Julenisse comes in the same way as he does in Norway.

On Christmas Day families enjoy their many beautiful greeting cards. Popular illustrations for Christmas cards in all Scandinavian countries may include stars, Julenisser, bells, Christmas trees, hearts, churches, and grain sheaves for birds. Danish cards carry their words for Merry Christmas—*Glaedelig Jul.*

On the day after Christmas, friends begin visiting to see the beautifully decorated trees. They also admire the blue and white porcelain

Juleaften plates which form a part of Danish decorations.

Long ago rich families gave their servants fancy plates full of cakes and cookies each Christmas. These plates were finer and prettier than anything the poor servants had, so they used them for Christmas decorations. In time, all Danish people decorated their homes with special Christmas plates.

In 1895 Bing & Grondahl, a porcelain factory in Copenhagen, manufactured the first Christmas plates for sale. Other companies followed the custom, but plates with the B & G initials are the most famous. Each year a famous artist is chosen to design the plates. On Christmas Eve the mold is destroyed so that no two years will have the same design.

Their designs show pictures of Danish scenes and holiday customs. Among them are: *Going to Church on Christmas Eve; Horses Enjoying Christmas Meal in Stable; Church-bells Chiming in Christmas; Lighting the*

At Christmastime some Danish children visit
Julenisse at a department store.

Candles; Christmas Meal of the Sparrows.
Many of these Juleaften plates are exported
and sold in the United States and other
countries.

Another of Denmark's contributions to the
world is the Christmas seal. The idea came
to a Danish postal clerk, Einar Holboell, as
he stamped Christmas mail in 1903. Holboell
worried about the many children who suffered
from the dreaded lung disease, tuberculosis.
Why couldn't a special Christmas stamp be
sold to help them, he wondered. The King
of Denmark liked the idea, and the following
year over four million stamps, or seals, were
sold.

Jacob Riis, a Danish immigrant who gained
fame in America, noticed the stamp on a
letter from his mother in Denmark. He wrote
a magazine story, "The Christmas Stamp,"
and popularized the custom in the United
States. Today Christmas seals are sold all
over the world.

4. Sweden

Luciadagen, St. Lucia's Day, is the forerunner of Jul in Sweden. It is sometimes called Little Christmas.

Every year Swedish children hear again the lovely Lucia legend. There once lived in the Roman Empire a rich and beautiful Christian maiden named Lucia. This was during the early days of Christianity, when Roman officials punished anyone who adopted the Christian faith.

Lucia refused to marry a pagan, and her angry suitor reported to officials that she was a Christian. Lucia was tortured and her eyes blinded. Still she refused to give up her faith.

She was put to death, and years later made a saint. Her name Santa Lucia comes from the Latin words *sanctus,* saint, and *lux,* light.

Christian teachers took the Lucia story to Sweden.

Because her feast day fell near the winter solstice, Lucia was made a symbol of victory over darkness—the Swedish Queen of Light.

In Italy Lucia had been pictured as a blind girl with a lamp, the patron of blind people. Sweden gave her a new image, based upon another legend. Long ago, says the legend, there was a famine in Sweden. It was then that Lucia came to the country, bringing food and drink to the hungry people. She stepped across the frozen lakes, dressed in shimmering white and wearing a crown of light.

Each year Swedish families choose a daughter to be the Lucia Queen. "Lucia costumes" are sold in stores.

Before dawn on December 13, the Lucia Queen dresses in a flowing white gown trimmed with a red sash. She wears a crown made of greenery and lighted candles. From bedroom to bedroom Lucia steps, singing as she serves buns and coffee. Special Lucia buns are flavored with saffron, a spice which gives them a pretty yellow color. Small children sometimes follow Lucia as she serves.

The favorite song is an old Italian melody, "Santa Lucia."

> Night goes with silent steps
> Round house and cottage.
> O'er the earth the sun forgot,
> Dark shadows linger.
> When on the threshold stands
> White-clad, in candle light,
> Santa Lucia, Santa Lucia.

Each Swedish community now chooses a Lucia Queen by popular vote. Hundreds of girls compete for the honor. The winner must not only be beautiful, she must also be kind like the first Lucia. Wearing a crown of candlelight, Lucia rides through the streets on a decorated float. Lucia celebrations are also held at schools, offices, and factories.

In the days following December 13, Swedes make and buy their Christmas presents. Gift wrappings are often sealed with fragrant wax. An old custom calls for each gift giver to write a rhyme and send it along with his present. The rhymes are read aloud before the seals are broken.

On *Julafton,* Christmas Eve, everyone hurries home after church services to join in the "Dipping Day" ceremony. The family gathers in the kitchen where a big pot of pork simmers. Each person dips a piece of bread into the pot and eats it. This ceremony honors other winters of famine when poor people kept alive by eating bread dipped into thin broth. Families who keep the custom will have good luck, according to superstition.

The main feast includes a smorgasbord, with many kinds of fish, as the Scandinavians

Getting ready for a Swedish
Christmas—dressing in a
Lucia costume, baking cookies,
and dipping candles.

are great fishermen. There are also meat dishes, including smoked reindeer meat, breads, cheeses, fruits, and pastries.

After dinner the children excitedly wait for Jultomten to come riding by in his sleigh, drawn by *Julbokar,* the Christmas goat. Jultomten raps loudly on the door and enters. "Are there any good children here?" he asks.

"Ye-es!" children answer, watching his bulging bag of gifts, called *Julklappar.* The name for gifts comes from *klappa,* meaning to rap or knock. In days past friends would rap on doors and toss in "joke" gifts. The custom has stopped, but the name Julklappar, Christmas knock, was given to gifts.

Bells ring before dawn on Christmas morning, calling people to *Julotta,* the early church services. *"God Jul,"* "Glad Christmas," greetings float on the frosty air.

January 13 gives children one last chance for parties—King Knut parties. Children dress in paper hats and costumes used during

Julafton—a time for candlelight services

holiday celebrations and gleefully "plunder"
the tree of the last sweets. They dance one
last dance, sing one last carol.

On twentieth day Knut
We dance Jul out.

5. Finland

The Finnish people celebrate "Little Christmas," *Pikkujoulu,* in preparation for the big festival, *Joulu.* All during December they hold Little Christmas parties which include dancing, singing carols, and playing games.

Families keep the century-old custom of being freshly clean for Christmas. Everyone takes a *sauna,* the Finnish steam bath. There are nearly a million saunas in Finland. The family sauna may be a small cabin, or it may be built as part of the cellar or the bathroom. Piles of stones on a stove are heated until the temperature may rise above 200 degrees. Water thrown over the stones produces steam.

Bathers sit or lie on platforms, perspiring. There are three parts to a sauna—perspiring, washing, and cooling off. Finns cool off by rolling in snow, diving into a lake, or taking a shower.

After a rich feast children excitedly listen for *Joulupukki,* Old Man Christmas. He arrives in a sleigh from Lapland, in northern Finland. In olden days the Finnish gift bringer was called "The Christmas Goat." He dressed in a long fur coat, a hood-like cap,

a white beard, and a goat's mask. Today Joulupukki looks very much like the Christmas Man in other Scandinavian countries.

When he asks, "Are there any good children here?" parents report on children's behavior. If he is satisfied he will open his sack. Younger children who help hand out gifts are dressed up like Christmas gnomes.

The legend which gives Santa Claus his reindeer-drawn sleigh started in Finnish Lapland. This land at the most northern tip of Europe has over 200,000 reindeer and many Lapps depend upon reindeer herding for their livelihood.

Children in many countries believe that their gift bringers such as Santa Claus or Father Christmas live in cold regions above the Arctic Circle. Many of them send Christmas letters to Finland and Greenland. Letters addressed to Greenland, a Danish possession, are forwarded to Copenhagen. Denmark's capital city has volunteers who answer the letters. Sometimes they enclose one of Andersen's Christmas tales.

Children who send letters to Finland get replies from Helsinki, the Finnish capital. The letters are signed by Santa Claus, or by the Christmas Man to whom they are addressed. Letters usually tell how gnomes and other helpers scurry about in a great workshop preparing Christmas surprises for children.

Soon children will be able to see a real workshop in Rovaniemi, chief city in Finnish Lapland. A "Christmas land" is being built, where people in costumes will act as Christmas helpers. The gifts, reindeer, and other thrilling sights should become an international tourist attraction. All the Scandinavian countries attract many visitors during Christmastime because of the ideal conditions for skiing and skating.

A carol by Finland's Otto Kotilainen captures the magic of Christmas in Scandinavia.

When snow lies deep and ice rings clear
and dim the sun through the frost and rime,
    when bare and silent lies the forest,
      long gone the swallow to southern clime.
Then runs a warm breath through wint'ry weather—
    it's Christmas time, it's Christmas time.

6. The Story of *Yule*

Long before the birth of Christ, people in Britain called Celts celebrated Yule, the rebirth of the sun. Celtic priests, called Druids, dressed in long white robes. With golden knives they cut the sacred plant called "all-heal" that clung to oak trees. They sent twigs to each home as protection against evil spirits.

In the century before the birth of Christ, Romans invaded Britain and ruled for about 400 years. The Romans brought customs from their own pagan midwinter holidays—their love for masquerading and pantomiming, and the joy of gift giving.

After the Roman soldiers left, Germanic tribes called the Angles, the Saxons, and the Jutes invaded Britain. The Angles gave their own name to "Angle-land" or England. The Saxons gave the lovely name of "mistletoe" to the all-heal plant. Another plant they dearly loved was holly, which grew better in England than in most places.

Jesus was born during these centuries of invasions, and December 25 was adopted as the date for celebrating His birthday. In the 600's a Roman monk, Saint Augustine, brought missionaries to spread Christianity to the English. More people began to celebrate Jesus' birthday. Special masses were held in churches, and the feast became known as Christ's Mass, later Christmas. It was a solemn holiday.

Viking ships sailed to Britain in the ninth century, and Danish warriors attacked the land. Some Scandinavians settled in England, Ireland, Scotland, and Wales. At one time

King Knut, spelled Canute in English, ruled Britain as well as Denmark. The Scandinavians brought their gods and legends, along with such customs as the Jul log and the boar's head. Christmas became less solemn.

Meanwhile, northern tribes, called Normans, raided France and settled Normandy. The Duke of Normandy, William the Conqueror, led the famous Norman conquest of Britain. He was crowned king in Westminster Abbey on Christmas Day, 1066.

Norman-French culture, which was more advanced, began to influence British customs. The Normans built or planned some of the grand castles and cathedrals which later played an important part in British Yule festivals.

The colorful folk customs from the Celts, Romans, Scandinavians, and French all blended together. Yule developed into a grand and merry festival with twelve days of continuous singing, feasting, and frolicking.

Bringing in the Yule log—and a small boy!

Caroling and the Christmas crèche, introduced during the Middle Ages, added to Yuletide joy. The crèche, or manger scene, dramatized the Christmas story in a way that everyone could understand. Singers called "Waits" caroled each Yule, passing along the songs by word of mouth.

Big bells in cathedral towers and handbells in the streets rang during the Twelve Days. Britain became known as "The Ringing Isle."

Royalty who lived in castles decked with holly, ivy, and mistletoe, held open house. Kings and noblemen feasted on boar's head.

Yule logs blazed in fireplaces. Noisy parades and pantomimes added to the fun and nonsense. Actors called "mummers" dressed in gay nonsensical costumes and gave merry Christmas plays.

In the 1600's, the Puritans came to power and banned merry religious festivals. However, the customs were revived later, and Yule became a season of goodwill. Children and poor people played bigger parts in celebrations. In the 19th century the Christmas stories of Charles Dickens helped to fashion this "new Christmas." So did the introduction of the Christmas tree from Germany. German-born Prince Albert, husband of Queen Victoria of England, helped to popularize this custom of his homeland.

About the same time an Englishman, Sir Henry Cole, began the custom of sending Christmas cards. Greeting cards, like Christmas trees, helped to spread the idea of Christmas celebrations all over the world.

7. England

Yule! Yule!
Three puddings in a pool;
Crack nuts and cry Yule.

Author Unknown

Preparations for the Yuletide plum pudding begin with Advent. Children help to chop the raisins, almonds, currants, and other ingredients. The mixing is often quite a ceremony, with everyone singing carols and taking turns at stirring "for luck." As each person stirs he makes a wish. A small silver trinket or coin placed in the pudding is supposed to bring luck to the finder.

By mid-December, Christmas trees are seen in public parks and churches. The American community-tree custom has now become very popular in Britain. Crèches are often placed under trees in churches. Children and adults leave gifts for the poor beside the trees.

England's most famous community tree is the annual gift sent from Norway. The magnificent tree towers in a place of honor in London's Trafalgar Square.

English families sometimes use red and green balloons for Christmas decorations, along with holly and mistletoe. The red-berried holly has inspired many English poets. For example, Christina Rossetti wrote:

> But give me holly, bold and jolly,
> Honest, prickly, shining holly;
> Pluck me holly leaf and berry
> For the day when I make merry.

The kissing bough adds color and excitement to homes. It is made of evergreens and trimmed with fruits, berries, and ribbons, with a bunch of mistletoe hanging beneath. Any girl caught under a kissing bough cannot refuse a kiss.

"You should hear our bells and caroling at Christmas," Englishmen tell visitors. Trained glee clubs sing to raise money for charity. Children carol for treats. Some of the most beautiful carol services in the world are heard in England's old cathedrals.

In the industrial city of Coventry, the old cathedral was destroyed by bombs during World War II. Still the people held their carol service amid the ruins. In the new Coventry Cathedral, a beautiful moment comes when lights are dimmed and the choir sings "The Coventry Carol." This lullaby for the Christ Child is from a 15th century Christmas play.

> Lully, lulla, thou tiny little Child,
> By, by, lully, lullay, thou tiny little Child,
> By, by, lully, lullay!

Singing carols at Yuletide in
Westminster Abbey and at a
friendly front door

England's most beloved carol service is the "Festival of Nine Lessons and Carols." Bible verses telling the Christmas story alternate with the singing of nine old carols. Each Christmas Eve a famous Nine Lessons service is broadcast from King's College, Cambridge.

The sound of bells is everywhere at Yuletide. On Christmas Eve the bells of St. Paul's Cathedral, the biggest bells in England, boom out the coming of Christmas. Shortly after, the bells of Westminster Abbey peal joyfully. Other bells, rung by expert bell ringers, take up the message. Handbells are rung by carolers singing through the streets.

Charles Wesley, the English hymn writer, heard Christmas bells as he walked across the fields to church in the 1700's. He drew an envelope from his pocket and began to write the carol, "Hark! the Herald Angels Sing."

Wesley later became a famous preacher, and taught his carol to people wherever he went. It is now sung around the globe.

Alfred Tennyson listened to Christmas bells and wrote "Voices in the Mist."

The time draws near the birth of Christ;
The moon is hid, the night is still;
The Christmas bells from hill to hill
Answer each other in the mist.

Weeks before Christmas, young children write letters to their gift bringer, Father Christmas, listing their wishes. Often they toss their letters into a fireplace. If they go up the chimney, the children say that the writer will get his wishes. If the letters do not burn, the children make new lists.

On Christmas Eve they hang up their stockings over fireplaces or at the ends of their beds. Father Christmas leaves gifts while children sleep, just as Santa Claus does. Many English parents decorate their tree after children are in bed, as in Scandinavia.

The Royal Family usually spends Christmas in one of their country houses, Sandringham.

A roomy fireplace is a good spot for hanging
Christmas stockings in almost any land.

The English princes and princesses have allow-
ances like many ordinary children and save
money to buy presents for everyone in the
family. About two o'clock on Christmas Day,
Queen Elizabeth II broadcasts Yuletide greetings to all the British Isles.

Most English families begin their feasts
about noon on Christmas Day. Dinner may
last for several hours with many courses.
Roast turkey with chestnut dressing is the

main course, though some families eat goose, duck, or chicken. The big moment comes when the plum pudding is brought in. It is traditionally decorated with holly and flaming from brandy poured over it and then lighted. A rich fruitcake is served for teatime in late afternoon, and small mince pies are served to visitors and carolers.

After dinner, children have fun pulling their "Christmas Crackers," and making them explode. These are similar to American birthday favors, or snappers, with little trinkets and surprises inside.

December 26, St. Stephen's Day, is called Boxing Day. On this day boxes of gifts and money were once given to servants and to the poor. Now Englishmen give gifts to service people such as postmen, mailmen, milkmen, and newsboys.

Boxing Day is also a day for sports, especially fox hunting. More than 200 packs of foxhounds take part in the Boxing Day meets.

Children go with parents to see the red-coated huntsmen, the fine horses, and the yelping hounds. Horse racing, car racing, and football games are other traditional events.

Boxing Day officially opens the circus season. The evening before opening day, people are invited to an impressive religious service called "The Blessing of the Circus." Clowns, acrobats, animals, and other performers in costumes all parade in the circus ring.

Christmas crackers make a loud noise and have a nice surprise inside.

Pantomimes are as much a part of the English Christmas as plum pudding. These pantomimes are dramatizations of nursery rhymes or favorite fairy tales such as *Cinderella, Peter Pan,* and *Aladdin.* Modern jokes have usually been added, and there is much clowning and nonsense.

Twelfth Night brings gay parties to end the Yule season. Men in some of the apple-growing regions perform an old ceremony, "Wassailing the Apple Trees." The term "wassail" means "To your health!" Bands of men circle the apple trees, singing old wassail songs. They carry apple cider, drinking some and pouring the rest over the tree roots. In olden days this was done to ward off evil so that trees would bear crops of big apples.

Every twig, apples big!
Hats full, caps full,
Three score bushels full,
Barns full, sacks full,
And my pockets full too. Hurrah!

8. Scotland and Wales

Christmas celebrations throughout the British Isles are much the same. Scotland, Wales, and Ireland have a few different customs though.

When the Puritans banned Christmas merriment, Scottish people kept their gay customs but made them part of New Year's Eve fun. This is why their New Year's Eve celebration, called *Hogmanay*, is still as big a festival as Christmas.

Crowds gather to await "the chappin o' the twal," the striking of twelve o'clock. As the church bells chime the magic hour, cheering, kissing merrymakers link arms and sing "Auld Lang Syne." This song was written by the great Scottish poet, Robert Burns.

"Hogmanay!" young folk shout as they rush to firstfoot friends. A firstfooter is the first person who visits a home in the New Year. He can bring either good or bad luck, superstition says. Families often arrange to have the right person to firstfoot them. Girls might invite sweethearts, rich people hire servants, while grandparents like to have grandchildren firstfoot them.

A luck-bringing firstfooter must be darkhaired, though a few places now make him fair-haired. It is believed that the dark-haired symbol was chosen because so many of Britain's early invaders were blond warriors. A woman or a flat-footed person is sure to mean bad luck!

The firstfooter must never come emptyhanded. He usually brings coal, bread, or money as symbols of warmth, food, and wealth for the coming year. He may also bring evergreens, symbolizing long life.

After a kiss from the ladies and girls, the

firstfooter joins in Hogmanay fun. Feasting includes round cakes made of oats called bannocks. Gay Scottish reels and the Highland fling are danced to the wild music of bagpipes.

"Hogmanay!" masquerading children shout early New Year's morning. Housewives have oat cakes ready for treats when the children sing nonsense rhymes.

> We're only bairnies come to play,
> Get up and give us our hogmanay.
> Hogmanay, trol-lol, trol-lol-lay!

Many Twelfth Night customs come down from Viking festivals and use fire. In some sections people still hold a thrilling ceremony called *Up Helly-aa*. A Viking ship, large enough to carry twelve men, is dragged through the streets by paraders dressed as Norsemen. Bands play Norse and Scottish tunes as hundreds of torchbearers light the way to the sea. Torches are tossed onto the

A Viking ship and crew pause at water's edge.

ship, and everyone cheers while the burning vessel rolls into the water. Afterwards there is feasting and dancing.

Wales is called the "Land of Song." It is also a land of legend and poetry. Long ago Welsh minstrels sang the legends of King Arthur and his knights of the round table. King Arthur, a legendary defender of Britain during Saxon invasions, became a popular hero in Wales. It is said that the first Christmas celebration in Britain was held by King Arthur in the 500's, and that minstrels made that famous Christmas joyful with singing.

Wales still enjoys a singing, bell-ringing Christmas. Dylan Thomas, the Welsh poet, wrote of his childhood joys in "A Child's Christmas in Wales." He remembered the bells: "And they rang their tidings over the bandaged town, over the frozen foam of the powder and ice-cream hills, over the crackling sea. It seemed that all the churches boomed for joy under my window; and the weathercocks crew for Christmas, on our fence."

Festivals of music and poetry, called *Eisteddfods,* have been held since the Middle Ages. Poets and musicians compete for prizes and honors. At Yuletide, communities hold special Eisteddfods, or carol contests, to choose the best words and music for new Christmas songs. The winning song is sung by carolers, thus giving Wales more music each year.

In sections of Wales and England, the "hodening horse" still clanks his teeth to scare and delight young children. This animal was once a part of Christmas plays. The horse's head is carved from wood and made scary with dug-out eyes and hob-nail teeth. Two people under a sheet form the body and pull the strings which make the teeth clank.

When the hodening horse visits homes, he is kept out until he recites poetry. The house-holders recite poetry in return. After a "battle of poetry" the hodening is let in to join the merriment.

The Welsh carol, "Deck the Halls with Boughs of Holly" is often sung.

> Don we now our gay apparel,
> Fa la la la la la la la la
> Troll the ancient Yuletide carol,
> Fa, la, la, la, la, la, la, la, la.

9. Ireland

And the lark said in her song,

    Often, often, often,

Goes the Christ in the stranger's guise;

    Often, often, often,

Goes the Christ in the stranger's guise.

Celtic Rune.

On Christmas Eve, just before sunset, an Irish father sets a candle in the front window of his home. The youngest child, in honor of the Christ Child, lights the candle. All over Ireland candles glow in windows throughout Yuletide.

At midnight great crowds fill the cathedrals for the Christmas Mass. The Roman Catholic faith remains strong in Ireland, except in Northern Ireland which is mainly Protestant like England, Scotland, and Wales.

Centuries ago, English authorities tried to stamp out Catholicism in Ireland. Priests hid in caves and forests, and visited homes secretly at night. Every family longed for a priest to arrive and say the Christmas Mass. Candles glowed in windows to guide priests to the right homes.

The Irishmen, who have always been wonderful storytellers, made up legends to explain the candles. "The candles welcome the Christ Child who returns each Christmas in the guise of a stranger," they said. Another legend said, "Candles light the way for Mary and Joseph who come seeking shelter for the Holy Babe." In some families each person has his own candle, decorated with a bright ribbon and holly.

The Feast of St. Stephen, December 26, is an important part of Yuletide. St. Stephen, a follower of Christ, was stoned to death by his enemies. To honor his death, men and boys once hunted wrens and stoned them. They dressed in bright costumes and held noisy parades, carrying the dead birds on branches of furze, a prickly evergreen shrub.

The wren "boys" of County Kerry making merry.

Many legends explain why the tiny wren was hunted. One says that during the Danish invasions, Irish soldiers planned a surprise attack upon the invaders. Just as Irish troops crept toward the sleeping Danes, a wren flew down and pecked at crumbs on a drum. The Danish drummer boy awoke, beat an alarm, and the Irish were defeated.

Another legend tells how St. Stephen, hunted by enemies, hid in a furze bush. A wren fluttered among the furze branches, and the enemies found St. Stephen.

Today's children carry toy or stuffed wrens on holly branches or in cages. They sing "wren-songs" to beg pennies for parties.

The wren, the wren, the king of all birds;
On St. Stephen's Day was caught in the furze;
Though his body's small, his family's great,
Put your hand in your pocket and give us a treat.
Sing holly, sing ivy, sing ivy, sing holly . . .

Old mummer plays are still given in Dublin and other parts of Ireland. The plays usually

end with an old carol to wish everyone a
Merry Christmas and a Happy New Year.

God bless the master of this house
Likewise the mistress too,
May their barns be filled with wheat and corn,
And their hearts be always true.
A merry Christmas is our wish
Where'er we do appear;
To you a well-filled purse,
A well-filled dish
And a happy bright New Year.